# GRaFfiti

## Devotions for Guys

W9-CTB-427

# GRaFfiti

## Devotions for Guys

## J. DAVID SCHMIDT
## with JOEY O'CONNOR

Fleming H. Revell
A Division of Baker Book House
Grand Rapids, Michigan 49516

© 1983 and 1998 by J. David Schmidt

Published by Fleming H. Revell
a division of Baker Book House Company
P.O. Box 6287, Grand Rapids, MI 49516-6287

Printed in the United States of America

All rights reserved. No part of this publication may be reproduced, stored in a retrieval system, or transmitted in any form or by any means—for example, electronic, photocopy, recording—without the prior written permission of the publisher. The only exception is brief quotations in printed reviews.

**Library of Congress Cataloging-in-Publication Data**

Schmidt, J. David (John David)
    Graffiti : devotions for guys / J. David Schmidt ; with Joey
O'Connor. — 2nd ed.
    p.    cm.
    Summary: More than fifty discussions, each with a relevant Bible
verse, on topics such as accepting defeat, respecting yourself and
others, living in today's culture, sexual temptation, and other
aspects of daily life
    ISBN 0-8007-5664-9
    1. Teenage boys—Prayer-books and devotions—English.
[1. Prayer books and devotions. 2. Christian life.] I. O'Connor, Joey,
1964– . II. Title.
BV4855.S35      1998
242'.632—dc21                              98-5998

Scripture quotations are taken from the HOLY BIBLE, NEW INTERNATIONAL VERSION ®. NIV ®. Copyright © 1973, 1978, 1984 by International Bible Society. Used by permission of Zondervan Publishing House. All rights reserved.

For current information about all releases from Baker Book House, visit our web site:
                 http://www.bakerbooks.com

*Before you read this book, read this page.*
You may be saying, "Here's another one of those dumb devotional books my mother buys for me."

But do you know what? Your mom, or whoever bought you this book, just might have finally come through for you.

This is one of those devotional books that doesn't require you to do a homework assignment every time you pick it up. You don't have to make any lists, write any poems, or say any cute prayers. All you have to do is grab your Bible, this book, and maybe a soft drink, and find a comfortable place to read.

God will do the rest, because this book has you in mind. It doesn't try to give easy answers to the big questions in your life.

What it does try to do is help you see that the Bible is not as heavy and complicated as you might think. I hope you will also see that it doesn't have to hurt to be a Christian.

Oh, yes, one more thing: For what it's worth, I've been where you are. I've fallen asleep trying to read my Bible, picked up my share of dirty magazines, and felt like a first-class jerk. But if you're willing to give him a shot at it, God can and will help you in your life. I hope as you read this book you'll see what God can do for you.

J. David

# Where It's At!

# Don't $ Buy the Lie

**one**

**1**

Basketball legend Wilt Chamberlain claims to have had sexual intercourse with more than two thousand women during his years in the NBA. Football star Michael Irvin has been charged with repeated sexual offenses. The list goes on and on.

All too often, the sexual exploits of today's athletic "heroes" hit the news. You hear everywhere that your personal fulfillment and manhood is measured by the number of women you have sex with or how many toys you buy. It's all a lie. The Beatles said in the 1960s, "Money can't buy me love," but nobody believed them. *Money still can't buy love.* It simply can't be done.

**Read Proverbs 7, about the consequences of buying love.** The movies and other media don't tell about the unwanted babies, lost self-respect, venereal disease, and pain that accompany trying to buy love. The Bible says, if you want to find the road to hell, look for the people who are buying and selling love. The Bible also says in 1 Corinthians 6:12–20 that when you try to buy love, you sin against your own body. The results are often more disastrous than with other sins.

God has a better idea. It can be summed up in one word—*purity*. Purity is not a state of perfection. It is a state of mind and heart that affects how you behave. It's not just about how you act with girls, either. It's something God wants you to work toward. If you watch what you read, what movies you go to, and who your friends are, and you ask God to help you *every day* to be pure, you will find that your batting average is going to go up. You may not think so sometimes, but you can be pure if you live in God's strength, not yours. You are worth too much to God and yourself to use your money, time, and energy to buy love. Don't buy the lie that sex, money, fame, and fortune will make you happy. You'll be tempted to buy the lie. Everyone is. Ask God to help you keep discovering that real fulfillment and meaning are found in him.

## Get a Grip

Get a Grip
Get a Grip

Can you think of a message you have seen or heard this week about some way that you can buy love? Do you see what was being promoted? A product? A way of life? Ask God to help you see what is behind the hype. Do not believe the lie in these messages.

Win at All Cost$?

two 2

At age twenty, Tiger Woods earned a cool $750,000 in his first six weeks as a professional golfer. *Not bad for a few chips and putts.* And what about the Shaq's $120-million contract with the Los Angeles Lakers? Albert Belle became baseball's first $10-million man when he signed on the dotted line for a five-year, $50-million contract with the White Sox. *Ka-Ching! Ka-Ching!*

When you look at professional player contracts and what they get for product endorsements, it's clear just how important winning is in our society. Defeat is no fun. It's an obstacle to anyone who wants to win. But should winning be *that* important? Should winning at all costs be the goal of everything you do? Are some victories more important than others? Or are some battles not worth fighting? **Let's look at what the Bible has to say about winning at all costs in 2 Samuel 11.**

On the surface, David looked like a winner. He not only got away with sleeping with Bathsheba, but he also was able to cover up the plot to have her husband, Uriah, killed. But David blew it. He forgot that God saw what he had done. Eventually David's sins were exposed and what looked like a victorious cover-up turned into tragedy. David's honor was tarnished, his daughter raped, and his son killed. It was only after all this and David's humiliated repentance that there was any "victory" for David.

David and his family definitely paid a high price for his desire to win at all costs. We can learn from his story that some defeats are more important than others. To see whether a defeat is important, ask yourself, "Will it matter a year from now?" Defeat can teach you a lot. Putting some of the smaller defeats in life into perspective will help you handle losing, and it will tame a hypercompetitive attitude.

David really messed up his life for a time. Yet, because his heart was right, God forgave him and built his character in the process. Maybe you've lost some pretty big battles in life. You don't have to live forever with those defeats. Jesus said to come to him if you are weary (of defeat), and he will give you rest (Matt. 11:28). If you involve God in your struggles, he will turn those defeats into constructive building blocks. You probably won't sign a multimillion-dollar contract, like Tiger Woods, the Shaq, or Albert Belle. You can develop a Christ-like character that doesn't have to win at all costs.

## Get a Grip

In what area of your life do you have a hard time accepting defeat?

What one lesson can you learn from a recent defeat?

three 3

# NO No Fear aahhhhhh!

Fear
is a billion-dollar
business. Every year in the
United States, Hollywood makes millions
of dollars producing movies with blood, guts, and an
assortment of body dismemberments. Halloween is a money-
making monster. We spend an estimated $1.5 billion on masks,
costumes, candy, and haunted houses. Even amusement parks,
such as Knotts "Scary" Farm in Southern California, turn their
entire facilities into one huge screaming haunted house for
October. Sellout crowds slap down big bucks for the privilege
of being scared out of their fear-filled minds.

Most guys rarely, if ever, admit to being afraid. Showing
fear is not cool. If you admit that you are afraid sometimes,
you will be laughed at. You've seen the shirts and hats with
the "No Fear" label. That about sums up the attitude we are
"supposed to have."

But this attitude is itself a Halloween mask. Everyone feels
fear now and then. Fear of being alone, of new situations, of
losing someone important to you; these and other fears are
universal.

**God has something to say about fear in Isaiah 41:10–16.**
When God created the heavens and earth, he did it simply by

speaking. Can you imagine our having the power and authority to create a whole universe just by opening our mouths and saying a few words? In Isaiah, God is speaking again. This time he's saying, "Fear not, I am with you." If God's words are powerful enough to create the universe, he is certainly powerful enough to back up the promise, "I am your God, I will strengthen you; I will help you."

Fear paralyzes us; it makes us panic. If we don't learn to contain it, it can spill over into other areas of our lives. God knew about fear's effect on our minds. That's why he made it very clear that we don't need to fear. God is always present and strong enough to help us—no matter how silly or how significant the fear may seem.

Get a Grip

What is the one thing you are most afraid of? God promises to help you face every fear.
Next time you fear, ask God to be with you and to help you. You can count on him.

# 4 four

# Carpet Bombing

During the 1991 Gulf War, the allied forces' strategic assault on Saddam Hussein's invasion army in Kuwait was a display of massive air power. In a relentless series of B-52 carpet bombings, hundreds of thousands of lethal bombs dropped on the desert. Iraqi casualties were heavy. Who could withstand such a terrible assault?

You may not be ducking for cover from B-52 carpet bombings, but you and every other teenage guy are being bombarded every day by blatant sexual messages in our society. Open up a magazine, and some slinky babe is wooing you to buy. Cable movies show lots of skin. Online temptation is only a few mouse clicks away. Magazines. Movies. Television. The Internet. Our society is saturated with sex. How can a young guy who wants to honor God stay pure in this sex-crazed world?

**There's an interesting account in Genesis 39 about how one young guy handled it long ago.** Potiphar's wife must have been some fox. How could Joseph not give in? *He ran.* What were the results? In the short run, Joseph probably was frustrated sexually. He was falsely accused and sent to prison. But God helped him with both troubles. The Bible says that God was kind to Joseph and gave him success in whatever he did.

Sex was then and is now one of the most difficult things to handle in life. There is no surefire plan for success over every sexual temptation. For men in their teens and twenties, sexual feelings are especially difficult to deal with. But God understands how difficult this part of your life can be, and he has a way to help you. You can learn from Joseph. He did the smart thing by running. By asking God to help, you can learn to run too.

Don't worry about your past failures. God can and will forgive you if you ask him. Look to the future and begin today to ask God to help you to run as Joseph did. Here are six ways you can run from sexual sin:

1. You can't help appreciating a good-looking girl. RUN from thinking sexual thoughts about her.
2. RUN by not even picking up a dirty magazine.
3. RUN by turning off a TV show that tempts you sexually.
4. RUN by not rehashing in your mind the comments made by friends whose standards are different than yours.
5. RUN by refusing to watch movies that you know are filled with sexual content.
6. RUN when your buddies invite you over to visit "certain" web sites.

The carpet bombing of sexual messages won't stop, but God can keep you safe from being vaporized by sin and guilt.

# Get a Grip

Get a Grip
Get a Grip
Get a Grip

Joseph ran away from sexual sin. By asking God to help you and doing your part, you can too. What one positive sexual standard will you hold to this week to honor your relationship with God?

# 5
## five
## Persevering
## through PAIN

Nobody likes to talk about sadness or pain. Even most Christians don't know how to talk about their overwhelming feelings of anger, doubt, grief, depression, or brokenness when death and sudden catastrophes enter their lives. Though painful, it's often easier to wear a fake smile and say that everything is okay instead of telling the truth about how you really feel.

In a broken world, pain and tragedy can and do happen. People, sometimes people who are outwardly good, die young. The painful result is that the world of their families and friends turns to hell. A buddy is cut down in a drive-by shooting. A family friend contracts AIDS. A soccer-player friend goes home one night after practice and hangs himself. Your dad walks out on your mom and family for some girl at the office. Your best friend gets a girl pregnant, then pays for her to have an abortion. Your mom dies of cancer. Inside you fall apart. This can't be happening. It *can* happen and does. You are left asking why.

Coping with the hurt and pain of life will be one of your toughest challenges. How can you persevere through the pain?

How well do you cope? What strength do you draw on? **God's Word has some encouragement when you hurt; read Isaiah 40:25–31.**

The last verse (31) is familiar to many Christians. Sometimes familiar verses lose their meaning or are used lightly. But a closer look at Isaiah 40:31 says three things about how to cope when things go wrong in life:

1. We gain strength by waiting. Waiting on God means asking him to help, then watching to see how he will do it.
2. This verse is a promise. God never has and never will go back on a promise. But it is up to us to believe it.
3. The strength God gives helps us to do normal things like running and walking through life. It also helps us to exceed what we thought possible ("fly like an eagle").

When something bad happens to you, your emotions get hurt. But to cope well, you don't need strong emotions. You need God to help you. You can persevere through the pains and hurts of life as you learn to lean on and trust in God.

## Get a Grip

Ask God to help you. *Believe* he will.
If God wrote you a letter about any pain you are
  feeling, what do you think he'd say?

# 6
## six
# Who Are you Following?

Pro basketball player Dennis "the Worm" Rodman is a leader. Forget about his rainbow colored hair. The wild tattoos. The nose ring. The painted fingernails. This guy has a bigger following than Moses leading Israel across the Red Sea. Sure, he's a basketball star and leader, but when it comes to his bizarre behavior, profanity-filled press statements, and his openly confused sexuality, where is he leading people?

Are you a leader or follower? Do you think you have the qualities to be a leader? Well, here's some good news. You don't have to be six feet tall, good-looking, dress in the right labels, or have a rich dad to be a leader. The qualities of leadership are not related to these things. **Look at what the greatest king of Israel told his son about the qualities of a good leader in 1 Kings 2:1–4.**

You may not play basketball like "the Worm," or maybe you're not the captain of the swim team, a student government leader, or a youth group president, but the qualities David told his son to seek are qualities you can develop too:

- *Strength:* Stay balanced physically in what you eat, and work to stay in shape.

- *Be worthy:* Command the respect of others because of your wisdom and because you also respect them.
- *Obey God's laws:* Obey the Ten Commandments to spare yourself a lot of hassles.
- *Depend on God, not yourself:* When life gets tough, remember that God works things out in life for his honor and your best (read Romans 8).

Leaders are made, not born; but one critical decision you need to make is whether you're going to be a leader or a follower. You can work on coloring your hair. You can get a nose ring or a tattoo. You can copy a superstar's best moves, or, you can do the really hard, important work of developing God's leadership qualities in your heart. If you involve God in the process, you can develop godly qualities that will run circles around Rodman's best moves.

## Get a Grip

Think of a leader you respect. What is the quality he or she has that you want in your life?

# 7
seven

# God@heaven.com

Ever get "bounced" by your friends? In e-mail and Internet terms, your message didn't get through. You got rejected. It's happened to all of us. You walk into the locker room after missing the game-winning point and your teammates can't look at you. You pretend you don't give a rip, but deep inside you really do. Missing the shot was bad enough. Rejection by your friends is like pouring battery acid on a bleeding wound.

The pain doesn't have to involve sports. You move to a new city. You're trying to fit in at your new school and youth group. Or, you just may be a loner without any friends. How do you feel when you're constantly left out? You wonder if you're going to face rejection and loneliness for the rest of your life. Will you always be left out? You know you need help, but where is it?

**Read Jeremiah 29:11–13.** This guy Jeremiah felt discouraged and alone much of his life. God had given him the job of telling the Jewish nation to get its act together—to get back to worshiping God. Jeremiah needed a promise he could live by when he got lonely. God's promise came out like this:

1. God has plans for you, for good, not evil. That means you aren't alone, even when you feel alone. Someone

smarter and stronger than you is looking out for your best interest.

2. God's plans will give you a future and hope. That doesn't mean hassle-free living. It means, whatever happens to you, God will bring good out of it.

3. God hears your prayers. Being part of a group at the time seems important. God knows your hurt or loneliness when that doesn't happen.

4. You can find God if you want to. The way to find him is simple enough—talk (pray) with him and look for him in the friendship of other people.

Loneliness is never fun, but knowing God is there and involved in your life can take the edge off your loneliness. By taking this promise and putting it to work in your life, you can work through your loneliness in a healthy way. Though God may seem distant and faraway in heaven, he is closer than you think. With God, you'll never get bounced.

## Get a Grip

What does it take to get God's attention? Review God's promises in Jeremiah 29:11–13. What kind of a future do you think God wants to give you?

# 8
## eight

# Outta the Question

Your buddy grabs your arm in the hallway at school and whispers something into your ear. "No way," you laugh, pushing him against a locker. Your friend gets back in your face and says, "I swear it's true. She told me herself. You're crazy if you don't believe me. You're also dumb if you don't do something about it fast."

You just found out that the gorgeous girl who sits across from you in your third-period history class has a crush on you. You've had your eye on her for a long time too. You're flattered, but you're also frustrated. By the way she talks, what she talks about, and who she hangs out with, you know she's not a Christian. You, your friends, and even your youth pastor have talked about it: She's off limits.

If you find this hard to take, you're not alone. As much as you may hate it, dating girls who don't personally know God is out. They are off limits—no good for you if you're serious about maintaining your walk with God.

**Read what the Bible says about this subject in 2 Corinthians 6:14–18.**

"How can one simple date with a non-Christian girl cause any hassle?" "No one falls in love by going to one football game together." "She needs me to tell her about the Lord."

That kind of statement is valid to a point. But you still have to come back to what the Bible says. The verses you read don't pull any punches. When it comes to dating and marriage there is no harmony between the believer and unbeliever. Some guys would say their values are the same as the girl's, but the bottom line remains: The Christian's purpose on earth is to please God, while the non-Christian's is to please herself or another person. You and she are going in two different directions. Waiting to find a Christian girl to date can be tough, but honoring God is worth the wait. Finding a Christian girlfriend, and someday marrying a Christian woman who shares your Christian values and love for God, will definitely be worth the wait.

Get a Grip

Do you feel God is being totally unrealistic about this issue? Why is it in your best interests to date someone who shares your love for God and Christian values?

Do you know someone whose relationship with God got messed up by dating a non-Christian?

What are the non-negotiable qualities of someone you'd like to date? Trust God to help you meet girls who share your faith.

# 9 nine

# Victoria's Secret

You just happened to pick up your older sister's latest *Victoria's Secret* lingerie catalog. As you flip through the pages, you learn the secret about what's inside. You may be tempted to rationalize your meticulous, page-by-page perusal of gorgeous women seductively posing in lacy lingerie by saying to yourself, "Hey, at least I'm not looking at *Playboy* or *Penthouse*." True, a lingerie catalog is not pornography, but what your mind does with its contents can have the same effect in creating a dangerous illusion about girls. It doesn't matter if it's an R-rated movie, an Internet web site, a late-night cable channel, a lingerie catalog, or hard-core pornography—whatever leads you to think impure thoughts can be dangerous to you and your concept of women.

**Second Timothy 2:22 readily admits that young men are troubled by impure thoughts.** One of the problems with sexually suggestive material is that its images aggravate your thought life at a time when it's very difficult to think clean thoughts anyway.

If you could see behind the scenes of the best-selling porno magazines, you would discover a team of technicians working over pictures with air brushes and computers. Their job is to remove any spots or blemishes on the pictures that would interfere with the illusion. The product is a perfect woman—or so they would like you to believe.

"So what? They still are fun to look at." The problem is that no woman will ever measure up to the illusion, not even the model who posed for the picture.

A steady diet of sexually suggestive material leaves unrealistic expectations of the imperfect real-life girls who have attractive qualities no pornographer is interested in capturing. Failure to adjust to the differences can ruin relationships and lives.

The Bible draws a clear distinction. Pornography, R-rated movies, and television shows heavy with sexual content reduce women to sexual objects. Reading dirty magazines or watching anything that causes you to lust is like keeping company with the wrong people. The Bible says to enjoy the company of people who love the Lord. It urges you to fill your mind with thoughts that build up yourself and others.

That magazine hidden in your room exposes you to dangerous and addictive pornography. This is a good time to recognize its effects on your life. Ask God for forgiveness and make a trip to the garbage can. Share your struggles with a trusted friend or your parents.

With God's help (if you call on him), you can avoid the pornography illusion.

## Get a Grip

Who are a couple friends you can talk with about staying pure? Together you can hold each other accountable to following God's way in this important area of your life.

# 10
## ten
# Don't Be Dissin' Me

The memory of gangsta rapper Tupac Shakur will be around for as long as his records continue to sell. Gunned down by unknown assailants, Shakur's controversial legacy lives on in his posthumous album, which became a best-seller the day it hit the stores. One of the main subjects rap takes to the street is the issue of respect. Black or white, gang member or not, respect is what every person wants.

Respect is not something that will just be handed to you in life. You have to earn it. As a man, you not only need to have self-respect, but you need to have the respect of those around you, men and women. Some guys have their own ideas about how to be respected by women. God has a different idea. **Read about it in Philippians 2:3–11.** Some guys would say you earn the respect of women by

- being tough
- being sexually aggressive
- making a good impression
- crying and expressing your feelings
- making good money

The Bible sees it differently. You earn respect by treating others correctly. That means

- being unselfish
- being real, instead of living to make a good impression
- being humble
- being interested in what others are doing
- having the attitude of Christ in serving others

You'll notice the difference in the two lists; the first promotes you and your accomplishments; the second (drawn from the Bible) builds up other people.

You can earn respect in life from those around you as you work to put them first.

## Get a Grip

Read Philippians 2:3–11 again. What are some things Paul tells you to do to have and give proper respect?

# 11

## eleven

## Lighting Up

Cigars used to just be a guy thing. Your dad or grandpa lit up after an evening meal or round of golf. Not anymore. Cigar sales have skyrocketed across America as men *and* women savor this smoky old pastime. Thanks to Schwarzenegger-size cigars, celebrity smokers, stylish cigar magazines, and classy cigar lounges, this hot new trend shows little sign of going up in smoke.

Don't be surprised if one of the guys pressures you to have a stogie. Giving in to peer pressure can get you into more trouble than smoking a single cigar. Learning to resist peer pressure is a critical discipline of the Christian life. Just as practicing your favorite sport requires discipline, it takes discipline to follow God's ways. God doesn't ask us to be disciplined people to impose useless rules on us. He knows that, without some discipline, we can never grow or refine our minds and our bodies. Peer pressure can make it hard to live a disciplined life.

**Take a moment to read 1 Corinthians 9.** Paul discusses self-discipline in this chapter. Without self-control and discipline, he implies, we can't live with confidence.

Are you struggling in your Christian walk? The first thing to check on is how regularly you read God's Word and talk to him.

You really can't expect to be close to him just by going to church on Sunday. Remember that Christianity is more than just a religion, and it's more than just a set of rules. It's a relationship with the God of the universe, who cares about you. He wants to spend time with you alone, so you can get to know him better, much as you spend time getting to know a friend. But unless you discipline yourself to take that time regularly, you're hardly even in the race, let alone near the front of the line.

By resisting peer pressure and living a disciplined, godly life, you won't see your relationship with God go up in smoke.

What is one area in your walk with God in which you would like to develop more discipline this week?

Do you have a strategy for answering your friends when they pressure you to go along with something you don't think is in line with a disciplined lifestyle?

# 12
## twelve
# HONORABLE
## Mention

Are you the kind of guy who always gets the vague and unsatisfying kinds of rewards? You know the kind—awards like "Best Attitude," or "100 Percent Attendance at Practice," or "Most Likely to Succeed (on Another Planet)," or the ever-inspiring "Honorable Mention." Oh, to be smarter, stronger, taller, better built, or better looking. With such pressure to win and succeed, it's easy to wonder what you're *really* worth when you don't measure up.

Your value as a person goes way beyond what you might feel you're worth. **Read what the Bible has to say about worth in 1 John 4:9–19.** When we don't believe in ourselves, because we lack self-esteem, we carry unnecessary baggage through life. Poor self-esteem makes you act cocky; you become terror-stricken to give a speech or ask a girl out. You drop footballs, fail tests, and hurt other people by your defensive actions.

Believing in your value is important to personal growth. To believe in yourself, you must understand what is really true, not superficial values of TV and the movies.

The verses in 1 John say something important about your value. Your worth is measured by what God was willing to do to keep you out of hell. God declared your value when he acted to give you a better life while you're on earth. When the Almighty God of the universe does something for *you,* it's worth taking note. In addition, he has given you talent and ability to do certain things well. In ways you never notice, he invests effort in your life. One thing to remember is that sin has a way of eroding your sense of worth. The more sin in your life, the easier it is not to believe in yourself.

If you are a Christian, God has drawn you out of a great crowd of people. He saw in you a worthwhile person whom he loved and could use. This makes you very valuable.

*You* may not be happy with how you feel, how you look, or where you came from, but these things don't matter to God. Nor does he care about your past. You are loved by, forgiven by, kept by, and encouraged to do good by the same God who holds the universe together. God's "Honorable Mention" list is different. Honor from God makes you an MVP.

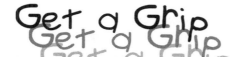

Everyone is good at something. What kinds of special gifts, talents, and abilities has God given to you?

Why do you feel less valuable when you compare yourself to others?

What does 1 John 4:9–12 tell you about how much God values you?

# 13

*thirteen*

# Piercing the Heavens

Pierce anything but your ears nowadays and you're bound to get some attention from your friends. Don't forget about the "attention" you'll receive from your parents when you sit down for dinner with a pierced nose or eyebrow.

Body piercing is definitely an alternative fad. But it seems that in the search for self-identity and personal meaning, piercing your navel, nostril, or nipple only brings a limited amount of temporary notice from others. You get God's attention through prayer—conversation with God. Body piercing may be strange, but many people have even stranger ideas about prayer and how or if God really answers prayer. **If you'd like some new insight into this whole matter of prayer, read Romans 8:24–39.**

God promised to hear us when we pray, but he did not promise to answer our prayers according to our wishes. This doesn't seem fair or right, does it? The thing to remember is that God knows better than you do what is best for you, both in the short run and the long run (for example, whom you should marry).

Although it may be difficult sometimes, you'll be much better off in life if you take everything to God and then accept the results. Whether God says yes, no, or wait awhile to your prayer, you can be sure that he has your very best interests at heart. You don't have to pierce any part of your body to get God's attention. Your prayers always pierce the heavens.

# Get a Grip

Take a few minutes and *write* a prayer to God. Keep in mind what Romans 8 says about your position in God and the assurance a Christian has. Does that change the way you approach prayer?

# 14
## fourteen

# Cross-Training

Eric Liddell was a gold medal winner in the 1924 Paris Olympics. His running career was portrayed in the movie *Chariots of Fire*. To the athletic world, Eric was best known for his 400-meter gold medal race, which no one expected him to win. His strongest event was the 200-meter race, which he declined to run because the event was scheduled on a Sunday. Though he faced strong criticism from the press, Liddell honored God by keeping the Sabbath, even at the cost of an Olympic gold medal!

The biography *God's Joyful Runner* describes Liddell: "Eric wasn't a man to spend his energy seeking worldly recognition; he was God's joyful runner, running out of love and deep desire for giving lasting glory to God."

Your commitment to Christ needs to be like that required for the endurance sport of cross-country running. With Olympic athlete Liddell, your goal as a Christian is to gain the prize of eternal life promised in Jesus Christ. While you are here on earth, your spiritual training is cross-training, picking up your cross daily and following Jesus.

As a cross-country runner in a tight race, you'd win because of abilities and training, not the abilities or training of the guy running next to you. Your team can cheer you on, but the race is determined by you alone.

Life is a lot like that. Family, friends, and the church support us, but the big decisions rest with us.

**Read Hebrews 12:11–13.** Any cross-country runner will tell you that learning to deal with pain is a major challenge. There is mental pain, which in a sense is false pain—it tells your mind that your body can't take three miles at this pace. That mental pain is an obstacle to overcome.

So it is in life. Our minds argue that we *have to have* something or someone. We give in to sexual urges, party all night, or drive too fast because our minds are asking for something we don't need or really want. How well you endure will tell you whether you will win over the temptation. The Bible says that at that moment we should think about Jesus and the fact that he endured temptation. We have a model to go by. Fixing our eyes on Christ and asking him for help, we have an inner strength to draw on.

Giving up a sexual thrill, anger, or a lie causes temporary pain. That pain comes with the territory of being a Christian.

---

# Get a Grip

The more you involve God in life's race, as Eric Liddell did, the more training you'll have for handling life's temptations.

What are you doing to train for the race that God wants you to run?

---

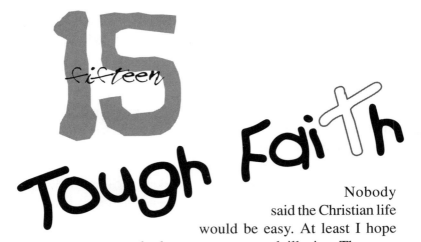

# Tough Faith

Nobody said the Christian life would be easy. At least I hope nobody gave you any such illusion. There are those who believe once you ask God into your life your problems will immediately disappear. The same mistaken sentiment teaches that God will answer every prayer like a waiter in a roadside diner. Sometimes Christians blame unanswered prayer on the one doing the praying. They say silly things like, "You just need to have more faith. You don't pray enough. If you were really following God, then you wouldn't have these problems." Those are easy words for someone else to say, but they offer no comfort and they are untrue. You don't need more faith. You may need to toughen the faith you already have.

It doesn't take faith to sit down in a chair—you can see whether the chair is likely to hold you. Real faith is shown when you don't know what the results will be. You follow God even when you can't imagine how things could work out. That's faith.

**Read Hebrews 11 to see how some people displayed their faith in God despite incredible obstacles.** Isn't it amazing how much faith Noah, Abraham, Sarah, and the others mentioned in this chapter had in God? They trusted him even when what they were told to do seemed ridiculous—even at the risk of being laughed at and ridiculed by their friends and relatives.

Some were beaten to death, but they remained faithful to the God they believed in. They believed that God had something better for them, though they didn't understand everything that happened.

This kind of faith isn't easy, and it doesn't come cheap. You may not suffer physically for knowing Christ, but you will have opportunities to display faith in him when it doesn't seem to make complete sense. Choosing a marriage partner or a college or deciding whether to move to a new town are decisions for which you will need faith. Hebrews 11 faith comes with confidence that God knows better than you do what is best for you.

Get a Grip

Your struggles toughen your faith. A tough faith that depends on God is exactly what you need to make it through this life.

Name a past struggle that has helped you develop a tougher faith in your walk with God.

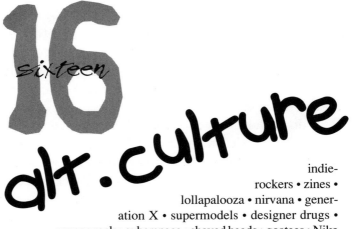

# 16
*sixteen*

# alt.culture

indie-rockers • zines • lollapalooza • nirvana • generation X • supermodels • designer drugs • grunge rock • cyberspace • shaved heads • goatees • Nike • piercing • no fear • Mortal Kombat • infantilization • hackers • green marketing • LSD • Howard Stern • Patagonia • wired • Oakley • gangsta rap • fat-free • snowboarding • muds

As great as it is to live in Western society, one force can be dangerous to your relationship with God. Popular culture has a major impact on how you think as a teenager. God wants you to use that grey matter inside your skull for what you choose to read, watch, play, buy, and listen to. Advertising, entertainment, television, locker rooms, classes, the Internet, and every other form of communication you can imagine convey the seductive messages of popular culture in their overemphasis on beauty, sensual enjoyment, and material gain. Popular culture will promise you anything you want, but it serves up nothing in return. God says that he has a better way.

In their proper places, there is nothing wrong with beauty, sensuality, or pride in achievement. Out of place, they devastate a Christian.

**First John 2:15–17 has some good thoughts on this.** On the surface, these verses sound as if Christians shouldn't enjoy life, and if they do, God is not part of their lives. If you get hung up there, you'll miss the real meaning. The writer of these verses seems to have energetic, fun-loving, and "with it" Christians in mind. These verses are not a one-way ticket to boredom and a restricted lifestyle. Rather, they are strong warnings to stay *balanced* and to be aware of the *popular thought* in your culture.

We live in a society obsessed with physical beauty, sex, and material possessions. Sadly, all of these good things God has given to man have been distorted and used wrongly. And the pressure is really on to think and behave like people who don't know God. The Lord wants to preserve you from the endless pursuit of what popular thought says is important.

Today, God can help you appreciate beauty instead of lust, keep sex in proper balance in your life, and realize that achievements and material goods are blessings from him.

What one thing in today's culture appeals to you but hasn't really delivered?

# 17

# Raising the Bar

How many people at your school went out for the high jump? Probably there were only a few, if any. Most look at the high jump and say, "Forget it. There's no way my body could clear that bar." Not surprisingly, a lot of teenagers feel the same about *holiness*.

You probably have a pretty good idea of what holiness is not. More difficult is the job of figuring out how holiness relates to your life. The very idea of holiness strikes terror in the hearts of most teenagers; surely God is going to take away everything they love to do. Holiness seems to be something for grandmothers, preachers and priests, bizarre cult leaders, and old T-shirts. After all, doesn't God keep raising the bar?

"If I try to be holy," you may reason, "then God is just waiting with a humongous checklist of things to eliminate from my life: no R-rated movies, no parties, no cruising, no dating, no, no, no, no. . . ."

**To get a more accurate understanding of this whole idea of holiness, read 1 Peter 1:13–25.** This is one of those spots in the Bible where the writer seemed to say something that is both confusing ("Be holy, because I am holy") and difficult to do.

How can you *be* holy like God when you can't see him or talk to him face-to-face? Well, one of the great things about the Bible is that it rarely says something confusing without also providing some nearby explanation.

Several keys for being holy are found in the first part of what you just read in 1 Peter. It gives three things to do:

1. *Prepare your minds for action.* That means *think.* Use your head and avoid *in advance* those situations where you might be tempted to do wrong.
2. *Be self-controlled.* This is a tough one for everyone. It means to stop kissing your girlfriend *before* it gets too heavy. It means go light on the gas pedal in the car when you're on the open road.
3. *Don't conform to evil desires.* Dig in and fight those attitudes or thoughts that you know hurt you and your walk with God.

Breathe easy. God is not out to make your life a drag. The guidelines he gives us about holiness in 1 Peter help us have the very best life has to offer. God's holiness is not like an impossible eight-foot-high jump bar you have to clear on your own power. He has set a high standard to live by, but he doesn't keep raising the bar. His holiness in your life is based upon his work and his power. Not your strength. All you have to do is *let him work.*

## Get a Grip

In what area of your life do you need God's strength to help you pursue holiness today?

# eighteen

# 18

# Rules Are Rules

1. 2. 3. 4. 5. 6. 7. 8. 9. 10.

Jack was expelled from junior high for bringing a broken air gun to school. Apparently, his school has a "no guns" rule and anybody caught with a gun receives an automatic ticket out the door. To make a long story short, Jack put the gun in his backpack, forgetting about the rule. He went to school but never took the gun out until he was on his way home. One kid saw it and told his mother about the gun. Mom complained to the principal. The principal called Jack's parents. Now Jack's out.

The principal didn't care that Jack forgot about the rule or that the gun never left the backpack or that it was broken. Rules are rules. *Seeya!*

Jack is a good kid. He's not a gangbanger, nor was he fearing for his life. Jack made a simple mistake that unfortunately had severe consequences. Jack learned the hard way that rules are rules.

We have considered how serious God is about making holiness a priority in our lives. God wants us to be holy, not to make life a drag, but so we can enjoy the freedom that comes from following his laws and commands. When we decide to ignore or forget to follow his commands, we eventually discover that there are consequences for our decision. **Take a**

**minute and read James 1:1–18.** Did you notice the pattern described in verses 14 and 15?

1.  Our evil desires tempt us. ("I'd sure like to go drinking just once.")
2.  If we give in to these desires, then we sin. (A six-pack later, you're plastered.)
3.  Sin leads to death. (If you drive, it may be literal death. If you do make it home safely, you feel like you let down yourself, your parents, and God. Soon you feel like death.)

Have you ever noticed how sin has a weird way of making you feel sick inside? Often when we sin, we suffer a deep disappointment in ourselves. This sense of disappointment comes from God. It is guilt and is designed by God to warn us when there is sin in our lives. You can pick any sin—drinking, anger, pride, lust, hatred, and so on. If you let it go long enough in your life it will hurt you inside. The best way to describe that hurt is death.

Rules are rules. When we break God's rules, we only hurt ourselves. God gives us his Word so we will know how to become holy as he is holy. And that is going to save you from a lot of unnecessary hassles in life.

## Get a Grip

Think of a rule God gave in the Bible that not only protects you from a lot of hurt but also makes you holy in his eyes.

# nineteen

# 19 The Burning Question

The burning question among most guys today (as for the past fifty centuries) is, "What does a girl really want in a guy?" Here's a sample of what girls from all over said in a recent survey for *Breakaway* magazine:

**Character:** I look for these qualities in a guy: good character (what a person is on the inside), a positive attitude, determination, patience, and the ability to stand up for what he believes. Kim.

**Jesus:** Above all, you must have a relationship with Jesus. Looks help, along with a good personality and a sense of humor. Guys, don't be cocky—that's a major turnoff. Ana.

**Respect:** I look for guys who respect me, know how to have fun, who call the day they promised, aren't stuck on themselves, love God, and think a relationship is more than just physical. Jennifer.

We can't determine exactly what a girl wants, but one quality you can develop should be important to a girl. **Read Titus**

**2:1–8.** One word stands out above the others—*self-control*. Self-control is one of the most difficult qualities to build and maintain in life. Everything in the world that is fun or feels good pulls us away from being self-controlled.

The Bible says self-control is a quality both men and women need. If this quality is needed by both, then it obviously is something important to others and ourselves. What does it look like? Here are some examples of what self-control is:

1. living a life that is balanced in how much and what you eat, whom you spend time with, and how you spend your free time.
2. reading the Bible when you don't feel like it.
3. putting a stop to kissing your date if it gets out of hand.
4. studying for a test when a good movie is on TV.
5. not swearing when all the other guys are.

Self-control is a quality you'll need all your life. It will help you get along with teachers and employers. It will help you stay faithful to your wife and to God.

---

## Get a Grip

How many and how much of the above qualities do you have in your life?

Ask the Lord today to help you see where you lack self-control. Then ask him to make you sensitive to his guidance at those moments when you have to make a hard choice.

---

# 20 twenty

# Faithful Friend

What do you look for in a friend? Someone who is loyal? Dependable? Willing to listen when you have had a bad day? What about someone you can trust with your doubts, frustrations, worries, fears, and complaints? A friend won't talk behind your back or turn on you by playing all sorts of weird mind games.

*Faithfulness*—that about sums it up when it comes to looking for a friend. Faithfulness is a character quality that distinguishes great friends from return-to-sender-type friends. Faithful is exactly the kind of friend God will be to you. God is looking for a friend in you and he promises to be a friend in return.

**James 2:21–24 talks about divine friendship.** Abraham was a friend of God because he *said* he would obey God and then *backed it up* with action. This same combination of believing in God and then acting on that belief can make you a friend of God's, too. Two things are worth remembering: First, faith isn't what you might think. "Just have more faith in God and you won't struggle with masturbation anymore."

48

These kinds of statements just aren't true. Faith is the confidence we have that something we want is going to happen. You need faith to believe in a God you can't see. Faith in God is the engine of your life. It motivates (moves) you to do right.

Second, faith isn't enough in life. You'll need to act right too. Right actions (driving the car of your life in the right direction) come from talking regularly with God (asking for directions), reading the Bible (checking the road map), and then just living (hitting the road).

Do you feel trapped by masturbation or something else in life? Combining faith that God can help you with the right actions (being careful about what you read and think) is what it takes to get you started out of a rut. It takes time to get out of ruts and habits. We don't get into them overnight. But as you have faith in God and do your part to act right, you'll begin to see progress. God is the most faithful friend you'll ever have. He is just the kind of friend you and all your friends need.

## Get a Grip

Can you think of a way God has demonstrated his faithfulness to you in the past month? Can you think of a way you have been a faithful friend to him?

# 21
## twenty-one
# Protective Gear

On October 12, 1996, Mike Cito, a center for Albuquerque's St. Pius X High School, wore a football helmet with a sharpened buckle during a game against the Albuquerque Academy football team. After five Academy players were injured by the sharpened buckle, Mike Cito was expelled from school and sentenced to one year's supervised probation, one hundred hours community service, and an 8:00 P.M. curfew. Not only was this seventeen-year-old charged with conspiracy to commit aggravated assault; his father was also sentenced for assisting his son with the crime.

When asked by the judge why he sharpened a buckle so that it would cut others, the younger Cito replied, "It was sharpened to protect me from harm. I did not know it would cause serious injury." (Right.)

Sharpening a football helmet buckle to protect yourself against harm is an extreme, dangerous, and—you guessed it—stupid thing to do. While few people resort to such crazy behavior, a lot of guys wear a different, "emotional" protective gear. You may wear all sorts of emotional protective gear to keep from showing your emotions. You don't want to get hurt. Maybe you were taught growing up that "big boys don't cry." You may assume that girls are more emotional than guys because girls openly show their emotions. That doesn't mean guys are *never* emotional. You may be afraid of looking like a geek if you show others how you really feel.

Everyone has emotions. It is healthy to show them. Instead of wearing protective gear on your heart or living in fear that other guys will think you're a wimp if you cry, it's good to cry when you feel sad.

How do you handle feeling down? Do you hide it? Pretend it's not there? **Psalm 139 has some promises worth considering when you feel blue.**

The Bible says God knows your thoughts before you think them; he knows when you wake up and when you lie down. When you were growing inside your mother, God was forming your body *and* your emotions. Whether you feel elated or depressed, God is guiding you, and holding you in his hand.

It should encourage you that from the moment you were conceived until you die, God has complete knowledge and control of your life. You will not always feel like God is in control, just as you won't always feel you are a Christian. Strong feelings mask the truth so that it becomes difficult to see what is real.

But your feelings don't change the facts. God knows you, understands you, and is actively at work on your behalf. You can count on this promise, no matter how you feel.

Don't resort to wearing protective gear on your heart . . . you'll only hurt yourself.

# Get a Grip

Your emotions are a gift from God and you don't have to feel weird for the way God has wired you. When was a time you just put your head down and cried—and you knew it was OK?

# 22
twenty-two

# Experimental Living

Bio-sphere 2 was a two-year experiment in which eight human beings lived together in the Arizona desert enclosed in a three-acre, self-sustaining, glass-enclosed terrarium. This $200-million scientific experiment was designed to gain a greater understanding of the earth's ecological balance, but it was a complete failure. Though it was hailed as the most significant scientific adventure since NASA's moon landing, Biosphere 2 biodegraded into intense personality disputes, insect infestation, dangerous carbon dioxide levels, and an overgrowth of creeping vines. Nice way to spend $200 million, huh?

Do you ever wonder if God often looks down on earth and laughs at projects like Biosphere 2? Human beings, it seems, try to be smart . . . *almost too smart*. How smart do you figure God is? One of the words used to describe God's wisdom is *omniscience*. That word simply means that God knows everything, including how to create Biosphere 1 (earth).

God's incredible knowledge actually is rather important to you. **To understand more about God's wisdom, read Hebrews 4:12–16.**

Everything you have ever said or done—your sexual decisions, the tests you've cheated on, the lies you told your mom and dad—all are known to God.

Most of us do not live as if God knows all about us. We would probably live differently if we did. Someday you will have to give an explanation to God for *why* you lived the way you do. God can't stand sin in your life. He will work gently by convincing you through his Word and your conscience. He will work firmly through an event or disappointment to help you see your need to change an attitude or an action.

Because God is all-knowing, you can trust him with your life. Now that's smart living. God understands the absolute best route for you to take, so you can make life count by making a positive difference in others' lives for his kingdom.

Realizing that God is all-knowing should concern you and motivate you to live more carefully. But it should also help you breathe easier as you think about your future. There is no better place to be than the place where you must depend on an all-knowing God for direction. Involve God in your life. You'll never regret it. With God, your life will never be a wasted scientific effort in experimental living.

## Get a Grip

Why is it better for you to live according to God's wisdom than your own? How can you remind yourself today of God's constant presence with you?

# twenty-three

# 23 All Fired Up

When you look into the mirror, what do you see? Do you see someone who wishes to be someone else? Do you see someone who is fired up to be the person God has created him to be?

Almost every teenager feels inadequate. There is unrealistic pressure to be strong, sexy, studly, cool, athletic, and almost godlike in the uneasy quest to fit in.

"But what if I'm not handsome or athletic or talented like everyone else?" you ask. "How can I accept myself as God made me when it seems like everyone else is so much better at everything than I am?"

The challenge is to discover how God has uniquely made and gifted you. **See what 1 Corinthians 12 has to say about getting fired up by understanding your unique talents and abilities.**

We all have gifts and talents that can be used, no matter how small they may seem to us. This passage describes how important it is for each person (part of the body) to do his thing, so that the entire body can function well. That's why there's no reason to play the comparison game. God doesn't rate one gift any better than another. And he doesn't ask us to function in ways we can't handle. He just asks that we give what we have to him to be used for his purposes. Many of us spend a lot of time and energy trying to be something we're not. When we don't accept ourselves, we make it difficult for God to show his power through us.

You don't have to live a life of inadequacy and insecurity by feeling other people are better than you. You can live with passion and purpose by firing up for God with the gifts he has given you.

# Get a Grip

In what area of your life do you sometimes feel inadequate?

What encourages you most about this idea that you've been given some gifts to serve God and others?

List talents or gifts you may have. Pick one of these that you particularly like and ask God to develop the quality in you for his service.

# 24
## twenty-four

# Worth the Wait

If more than half a million teenagers can stand on the Mall in Washington, D.C., to pledge sexual abstinence, then you can do the same where you live. Since 1993, the True Love Waits campaign has had a tremendous influence in helping teenagers make positive sexual choices.

Each person seems to have an individual definition of *love*. Is it a feeling? A giddy emotion? A passionate sex scene like in the movies? Your challenge as a young person is to choose whose definition you will live by. If your parents are divorced, you probably wonder if love and sex and marriage are really worth waiting for.

**Read the well-known chapter in the Bible about love: 1 Corinthians 13.** Paul wrote this letter to people who lived in the wild and crazy city of Corinth, where love was almost completely expressed by sex—and bizarre sex at that.

> Love is certainly a feeling, but the feelings are not the most important part of love. Love is also action and motivation.
> Love is patient and kind. It waits for the bathroom without grumbling.

Love is loyal. It sticks up for a friend when he's not present to defend himself.

Love believes in someone. It encourages a friend to tell the truth.

Love expects the best from someone. It helps his date believe in herself.

Love defends. It says something good about parents, even though everyone else cuts theirs down.

Love is not jealous. It compliments a brother on good grades.

Love is not proud. It realizes certain talents are gifts, not rewards.

Love is not rude. It doesn't make fun of people who aren't as smart.

Love does not demand its own way. It would never say, "If you loved me, you'd sleep with me."

Love is all this and more. The highest definition is that God is love. Don't kid yourself into thinking something is love when it isn't. If you are wondering how well you love or if you are in love, try measuring your feelings against what the Bible says true love is. The results might surprise you. Even if you're not a virgin anymore, if you confess your sins to God, he is ready and willing to forgive you. He will give you the strength to make good decisions in the future.

Remember: True love does wait and true love is worth waiting for.

---

# Get a Grip

Have you made a definite decision about waiting for marriage to begin sexual intimacy? If so, way to go! Ask God to help you keep your pledge and find a friend who will hold you accountable.

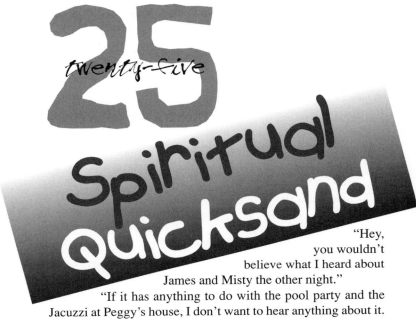

# 25
*twenty-five*

# Spiritual Quicksand

"Hey, you wouldn't believe what I heard about James and Misty the other night."

"If it has anything to do with the pool party and the Jacuzzi at Peggy's house, I don't want to hear anything about it. James just told me last week that he's on the student leadership team in his youth group . . . and just a month ago he was bragging about taking a purity pledge."

Have you heard a Monday morning conversation like this at your school lately? Throughout your life you will meet Christians who have different standards than you. Some Christians will say they have certain standards they live by, but their actions will show their *real* standards. Other Christians may be so strict that your standards (which seem pretty conservative to you) will appear loose to them. Some will say it doesn't really matter what we do or how we live since our sins will be forgiven. That line of thinking leads too many teenagers into spiritual quicksand.

**Read Romans 6 for some insight about sin.**

Apparently, the Christians in Rome assumed they could live any way they wanted and still be followers of Christ. They were betraying Christ by allowing sins to control them. And they were putting other things before God.

Sometimes we see sin clearly, because it's obvious. At other times, we slide in—inch by inch—and before we know it, we've taken a big fall. Sexual sin often happens that way. It seems so innocent and right at the time. But impure behavior makes us slaves to sin. It's much more difficult to do the right thing the next time, if you've allowed yourself to go farther than you should have on your last date. That's how sin traps us and makes us slaves. Before we know it, we're sinking in our sin. The compromises of spiritual quicksand thinking can suck us into trouble.

The Bible tells the story of one of Jesus' disciples who compromised his life so much that he eventually destroyed his relationship with God and then destroyed himself. Judas betrayed Jesus for thirty shekels, or about $19.50. It seems crazy. Yet we daily betray God by living selfishly, continuing in sinful behavior, and putting possessions or people before God. What about you? Don't allow little sins to suck you into the dangers of spiritual quicksand. Follow God's standard for right living and what he says about sin. Even if you feel stuck in sin, God promises to help pull you out. You can be a slave to sin or live with freedom in Christ. The choice is yours.

## Get a Grip

How do teenagers who don't make specific dating and sexual standards get in trouble with their sexual decisions?

What are your standards?

# twenty-six

# 26 Personal Trainer

In the battle for athletic scholarships, parents sometimes make sizable investments in their sons' and daughters' athletic futures. The latest rage? *Personal trainers*. Nowadays it's not enough to just show up for practice. If a student really wants to land that big scholarship, he or she needs a shooting coach, a strength coach, a pitching coach, or a batting coach to perfect his or her every move.

Whether or not you have a personal trainer, God is concerned about the physical aspects of your life. But God is more than a personal trainer. He is concerned far more about the condition of your heart, what you put in your mind and body, where you go, and who you share your body with.

**Daniel 1:8–21 and 1 Corinthians 10:31 have something to say about your body.** Daniel's life is a good example of what happens when a person honors God. God blessed Daniel with good health and the respect of others. Like an athlete who wisely listens to his personal trainer, Daniel benefited from listening to God.

In the New Testament, Paul gives us some personal training advice to help us honor God. What you put into your body and what you do with it should safeguard God's reputation and yours. Your body is a gift from God, and ultimately God is the final authority on personal training.

Take a minute right now and check yourself on the following questions:

Where have you taken your body in the past month? (bars, Bible study, gymnasium, running track?)

What have you put into it? (junk food, vegetables, booze, smoke?)

How much of your body have you shared with someone else?

How will body-piercing and tattoos glorify God?

Do you participate in dangerous stunts and risks like drinking and driving?

Keeping our relationship with God intact is the most important thing in life. How we handle our bodies can affect that important relationship. Handling your body carefully not only brings you self-respect, but pleases God.

## Get a Grip

Name one way you can glorify God with your body this week.

# twenty-seven

# Second Chances

Have you ever said to yourself after majorly blowing it, "That's it! God has had it. He can only forgive me so many times. I must be roadkill now." You think God is sick of giving you second chances. Even when you ask God for forgiveness, do you still feel guilty? Maybe you feel absolutely worthless. Deep inside your heart, you wonder if God does care about you anymore. Could he ever use you for something important after what you have done?

**Read 1 Timothy 1:12–17.** Consider this guy, Paul. Talk about an unlikely candidate for God's work. At one time he was directly responsible for killing Christians. He took it upon himself, before he believed in Christ, to track down Christians and have them murdered. But there is no sin too terrible for God to forgive. The Old Testament is full of stories of people who sinned against God—liars, egotists, cheaters, you name it. When they sincerely asked for forgiveness and continued following him, God forgave them and used their lives.

This doesn't mean we should sin just to prove God can use us. But since we all do sin, we need to ask him often to forgive us and keep us on the right track. God isn't looking for super people—he's looking for people who will acknowledge their sins and turn to him. They're the only people he can use.

What about you? Do you believe God can clear the slate and use your life? God is bigger than any sin you could ever commit—just look at the people in the Bible and see what they did. The God who loves and forgives you is the God of second chances . . . and third and fourth and fifth . . . *ad infinitum.*

Get a Grip

If God promises to forgive you, what is holding you back from receiving his forgiveness today? Think about an area in which you keep blowing it. Ask for forgiveness and the grace to change.

# 28
## twenty-eight
# uncommon sense

Stick a burrito into the microwave for a minute and what do you get? Dinner (or a mess). Flip on the television? Fantasyland! Go online? You're on someone else's server on the opposite side of the planet.

We take for granted so many things. We believe things will work a certain way, without even thinking about it. Lots of things we do in a day require us to trust. *Trust* is one of those words some Christians throw around or use lightly. "Just trust God" sounds great, but it can be tough to do.

**Jeremiah 17:5–8 has something to say about *where* to put our confidence.** These verses say, *Trust in yourself* and you will *find yourself alone* when big decisions need answers. ("Where should I go to college?") You will *find yourself without roots* when temptation hits. ("I really didn't want to go that far with her, but somehow I didn't have the strength to stop.")

You will face lots of little but important decisions and several big ones. How wisely you decide depends directly on whether you trust your own common sense or God's. The Bible promises that when we put our confidence in God, we become more *stable*. We *have less to worry about* when we face tough decisions.

Do you *trust* God by asking him to help you make wise decisions? You know, God's got common sense. By simply asking him to help you with your decisions, you can exercise and strengthen your confidence that God will lead you along the best paths. Trusting God calls you to use uncommon sense. For all the things we instinctively trust in every day, God is calling you to live according to his common sense.

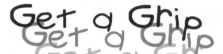

Walking in faith and trusting God feels like stupidity to the world. But God calls it uncommon sense.

How will you seek God's wisdom for an important decision this week?

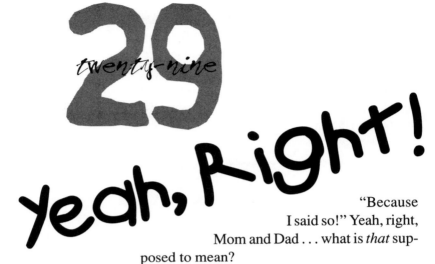

# 29
## twenty-nine

# Yeah, Right!

"Because I said so!" Yeah, right, Mom and Dad . . . what is *that* supposed to mean?

Remember Bill Cosby's parenting line: "I brought you into this world and I can take you out"? Then there is "Don't make me say it one more time," and the all-time favorite, "You're not going anywhere until that room is clean!"

Do parents take secret classes to learn to talk like this? Bizarre, completely vague responses like that can make you really angry. And parents are wrong for saying these things. But if you handle it emotionally, get mad or bitter, problems can escalate. The Bible has something to say about how we handle our anger.

**Read what Ephesians 4:22–32 says about personal growth.** The emphasis is on attitudes changing, truthfulness, and handling anger carefully. Actually, these verses are for you *and* your parents. When your parents say, "Because

I said so," and you get ticked, you have a responsibility to go to them and calmly tell them your feelings. You demonstrate godly maturity when you try to work out the differences. They should grow from your openness. You can strengthen the communication process tremendously. Ask God to help you be honest with your parents and to give you the right attitude about talking to them. As you work on your attitude and go to bed with a bitter spirit less often, you'll find that accepting some of the strange things your parents say will get easier. With God's help you can have a good influence on your parents and do your part to make home a better place to live.

Next time your parents say something that really ticks you off, what can you do to handle it God's way, not your own?

Unfortunately, even if you do your part, poor communication and other problem patterns may make your parents resistant to change. Are you willing to keep trying and praying, even if things seem hopeless?

# 30

*thirty*

# Get Me Outta Here

Despite everything you may see on MTV, hear on the radio, or read in your favorite 'zine, yours isn't the first generation to experience restlessness.

Especially if you're a Christian, you may feel it's a sin to feel restless. Since the time of Jesus, many sincere Christians have experienced periods of restlessness. Even Thomas, one of Jesus' friends, felt this way. **Read about Thomas's restlessness in John 20:19–31.**

Like Thomas we want hard, tangible proof that being a Christian is worth it. Jesus said to Thomas, "Don't be faithless any longer. Believe." Actually, believing in Jesus today is much harder than it was for Thomas. Computers and television have made us skeptical of the supernatural—of things we can't see and figure out. Not being able to figure something out leads to doubting, and doubting leads to restlessness.

Take some time to seriously listen to the lyrics of today's most popular musicians and groups like *Smashing Pumpkins, Pearl Jam, Nine Inch Nails, Alanis Morrisette,* and other alternative groups. They all speak of adolescent angst, restlessness, hopelessness, and despair, but what solutions are they really offering? Listen to enough music and it's easy to believe that God has abandoned the earth. Don't buy the lie.

Restlessness is a part of our culture. It will always be there as a force, pulling us away from important things, such as school and church and family. Like rebellion, restlessness can only hurt you if you don't channel it into something constructive, like a prayer to the Lord. If you are restless with being a Christian, take some time to talk to God. Open up and tell him what you feel. God is the Lord of every generation. He is even the Lord of your generation. Even when you are feeling hopeless about your future, God can give you peace for your restlessness.

What are you feeling restless about today?
Jesus talked to Thomas about his restlessness.
   Write down what Jesus would say to you about
   receiving his peace today.

# thirty-one
# 31
# Feeling Doomed

Your science teacher says, "Evolution is a proven scientific theory. The Bible is filled with mythical fairy tales about a creation story. It has stories to prove the existence of a so-called God."

One of your best friends says, "I can't understand how a loving God would let so many people, even children, suffer from starvation, war, and poverty."

At times, everyone has doubts about God. Does that mean your faith is doomed? Do your doubts mean that you don't love God? If there were some way to prove that Christianity is not real or that God isn't going to deliver on the heaven thing, you can bet a lot of people would live differently.

Do you ever wonder whether Christianity is worth it? If there really is a God who answers prayer? Doubts are part of the process of believing in God and taking him at his word. **The Bible has some encouraging words about belief in God in Psalm 8:3–4 and Hebrews 1:1–3.**

When you doubt, there are three things to think about:

1. It is extremely difficult to believe that all of the universe and especially the consistent order of things on earth came about without the intervention of a supreme intelligence.

The evidence is with the Christian, not the above science teacher. Consider, for example, the complexity of the human brain. Even scientists sometimes say that humans seem to be copied (an image) from something not found on earth.

2. The Bible is unique. No other religious book has withstood such criticism, and only the critics are proven wrong. It defies the odds. Nothing gives cause to believe that this Book is not what it claims to be—the official writing and history of the supreme intelligent Being who claims to have created the heavens and earth.

3. Believing and practicing what is in this Book changes people's lives. Putting faith in the God/Man Jesus Christ who is written about in the Book changes murderers and liars. It frees people from guilt. It gives people a sense of purpose in life. Psychology can't do it, science can't. No other religion so thoroughly revolutionizes a person as believing in Jesus Christ.

Doubts are part of life. Even if you're feeling doomed when you doubt, God can handle your doubts.

There's no doubt about that.

## Get a Grip

We often doubt God when we are tired, afraid, or confused. When are you most likely to doubt God?

If you're doubting, take some time to recount all the big and little proofs you have that God is real.

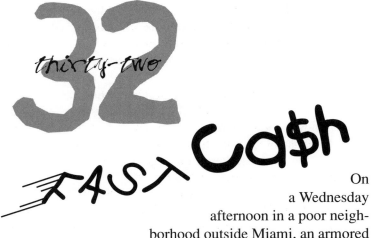

## 32
### thirty-two
# FAST Ca$h

On a Wednesday afternoon in a poor neighborhood outside Miami, an armored truck overturned and spilled hundreds of thousands of dollars in cash and coins over the street. Residents scooped up every dollar, quarter, dime, nickel, and penny they could. Within twenty minutes, over $700,000 in cash and food stamps was missing. Women even took off their blouses to fill them with money and walked off in their bras. People claimed that the overturned truck was a gift from God. Pennies from heaven. When a dozen police officers knocked on doors to recover the stolen money, the only thing people offered was blank stares and silence. Total turned in: zero.

If a Brinks truck overturned in your neighborhood, would you go for the fast cash? Or, would you go for keeping your reputation for having a good name? **Read Proverbs 22 and consider its advice about reputation.**

The Bible says here that you may be faced with the choice between riches and a good name. It's interesting that verse one sets up this choice. If a person's reputation is tarnished, it is most often because he or she didn't handle money correctly. But you may also have to choose a good reputation over a good time (sexually) or popularity (lying to cover for a friend).

72

This chapter also makes it clear that a good name is worth more than money, a good time, or popularity. Sometimes Christians have used reputation as a club to whip people into line. "If you mess around on a date, you'll get a reputation." "If you don't tell the truth, you'll get a reputation."

People do know us by how we act, but the real reason for living correctly should be to please God, not fear of what others will say.

You can always rebuild a tarnished reputation. God forgives and forgets your past mistakes. He wants to help you live right, so that you can rebuild or maintain a good name. When faced with the choice to go for fast cash or a good reputation, go for the second. In the long run, it's worth more than a truckload of cash.

Get a Grip

Why do you think it was easy for people to rationalize their stealing by saying that the money was sent by God?

What do you justify that might not be right in God's eyes?

# thirty-three

# 33

# NO Slackers

Slackers; they don't pull their weight. They never chip in for gas, movies, or pizza.

When Jesus Christ came into your life, he changed you, turned your life around, and gave you hope and peace. This process was no accident. God was in it the whole way, and he used other people to get the job done in your life.

There are all sorts of messages telling you what to think, believe, say, and do. Do you want to settle for an OK life? If you are a Christian, you have an exciting message to share that can change the lives of your family and friends. God's Word talks about the importance of sharing your life and the message of Jesus Christ with your friends and relatives so his work can be duplicated in their lives. Being a Christian is so valuable that we have the freedom and privilege to share it with others.

**Read Romans 10:1–15.** Generally speaking, there are two types of Christians: "silent witnesses" and those who hold evangelistic services at the bus stop. Neither extreme is appropriate all the time. The silent witnesses never try to share their new lives in Christ with others, and the *fanatics* turn people off. There is a middle ground.

Today, God needs people who know him and who are mature enough to say in public what they believe in private. Most Christian high school students can't share their faith in Christ with others. They fear being rejected or losing popularity. So they remain silent witnesses, while their friends have abortions, get drunk, and break the law. Here are some simple ideas on how to tell others about God:

1. You don't have to pray before lunch, but a regular quiet prayer lets friends know God is in your life.
2. Invite some friends to a Bible study. But be sure you have open discussion about what you read. Don't hold a church service.
3. If your church has a good youth group, invite your friends to an activity.
4. Ask your friends some questions about their beliefs in God. God can open up discussion among you and give you an opportunity to share your faith.

God doesn't need Christians who go around whacking people on the head with the Bible, but he also doesn't need slackers. God wants you to at least be willing to do something active to tell your friends and relatives about your new life in Christ. God is ready to help you and give you courage.

## Get a Grip

On a card, write the name of someone you know who needs Christ. Keep it on your dresser. Pray as often as you see the card for a chance to talk about God with that person. When he opens the door, walk through. He'll go with you.

# thirty-four
# 34
# God Talk

It's a language that's not commonly understood by the majority of the high school and middle school population across America today. If you've been in church or a youth group for any time now, you know what *God talk* is. It's spiritualized language that is religious gibberish to those who don't speak it. Worse, God talk can mean almost nothing to those who *do* speak it. God talk doesn't make anyone a better, stronger, faster, able-to-leap-church-steeples-in-a-single-bound, psalm-singing, spring-of-faith-type Christian.

Heard the God talk? *Born again. Filled with the Holy Spirit. Sanctified. Justified by faith.* Oftentimes these words or phrases can lose their meaning and become boring to you. So you know how non-Christians will react—the great tune-out. Christians shouldn't tune out explanations and applications about sanctification, for instance. If we do, we won't grow in understanding. Yet neither do we throw around these words around non-Christians as a spiritualized code. The way some Christians talk can be a real pain.

**The solution is found in 2 Timothy 2:14.** You can trust the Bible to say it straight. There will always be "religious" people who are into God talk. It is useless to quarrel with them inwardly (inducing bad feelings toward the church or people) or outwardly (arguing or turning people off). You won't change them, but you can do something constructive. The Bible says to do two things: Do your best to be presentable (win your own battles with sin) before God and be a person who knows how to handle God's Word, clear and relevant in how you talk about God and religious things to other people.

You'll never get away from religious God talk or the Christians who use it. How you handle these people will be a test of your ability to accept others and to apply what you know about being a better person.

## Get a Grip

How can you demonstrate your faith today in an honest, authentic way—without the God talk? Are there Christian expressions you use without thinking? Pick one and work on changing it or dropping it.

# 35

thirty-five

# Can I Trust God?

Do you have a hard time trusting others? Half of all the teenagers in America have experienced the divorce of parents. If you are one of them, you're probably skeptical of words like trust, commitment, vow, promise, and loyalty. It doesn't take long to lose faith in a friend who broadcasts a secret more widely than NBC. Putting your trust in God is definitely a scary step of faith when the most important people in your life let you down.

Can the Bible be trusted? When you think about it, Christians make big claims about the Bible. Christians say the writers of the Bible were inspired (directed in their thinking by the Holy Spirit) to write exactly what God wanted them to say. They also claim that we can trust God's Word to have no errors. We can trust its presentation of Christ and what he did.

Can you really trust a Book that was finished almost two thousand years ago to be true and of any value to you in your life? **Read 2 Timothy 3:14–17 three times out loud.** One verse in this passage says, "All Scripture is God-breathed." What proof do we have that the Bible came from some powerful God no one has ever seen? Here's something to think about: At least forty men, in thirty different occupations, wrote the Bible in three different languages over sixteen hundred years. In all, 807,367 words in the Bible work together in harmony to talk of one God, one devil, one heaven, one hell, and one way of salvation. The Bible has withstood wars, human criticism, and time to become the best selling book in history.

But more than all of this, the best proof we have that God's Word is trustworthy is the fact that reading, applying, and believing it can change our lives. Because what is in the Bible are God's thoughts and insights on how to make it on earth, it links us with a loving God. Many religions have a "holy book," but no religion has a book like the Bible, which, when believed and applied, can be of such hope and help. History proves that when people take God's Word seriously, it works. How about your Bible? Is it working for you?

Get a Grip

The mistakes of others can make it difficult to trust God—but not impossible. Remember that weak people can let you down—but God is not weak, and he does not change.

What one step of faith is God asking you to take to show that you trust him?

# thirty-six
# 36
# Good Advice

How many times have you heard parents say ridiculous things that are supposed to help but don't even relate to your life? Really dumb things like, "When I was a kid. . . ." How do you think they would like it if you stormed around the house wanting them to do things differently because, "When I was a toddler, this is how things were. . . . When I was in third grade, we did things this way. . . ." They'd probably shake their heads in amazement, just as you do now. What about when they ground you for walking in the door ten minutes late? *Grounded for being ten minutes late? . . . I'm calling my lawyer!*

Handling adults or parents is no small task for a teenager. Parents seem to have such out-of-date attitudes. They get hung up over little things like ten minutes or a messy room. The rules they want you to live by went out with hula hoops.

What's the best way to handle your parents, or any adult for that matter? **The Bible has some good advice in Ephesians 6:1–4.** This is a good passage to sit down and talk about with your mom or dad. There's something in it for both your folks and you. You'll notice that the Bible says that fathers should not exasperate their children. If you're feeling exasperated, you need to take the initiative and talk to your parents. Often teenagers have trouble with adults because of poor communication, not differences of opinion.

The important thing to remember is that God asks you to honor and respect your mom and dad, even when you disagree with them. Believe it or not, your folks have twice as much experience at living as you do. They've seen their own mistakes and hurts, and they want to help you avoid them. Don't let a disagreement over a movie, curfew, or choice of friends stand between you and your parents. Next time you have a hassle with them, whether you live with one parent or two, remember that God wants you to honor and obey them, not because "that's just the way it is," but because God has your best interest in mind. He provided adult guidance so that "it may go well with you" (Exod. 20:12).

In what areas can you show more responsibility, and so earn your parents' trust?
If problems with your parents are deep and seem to be unresolvable, is there a pastor or other mature Christian from whom you can get counsel?

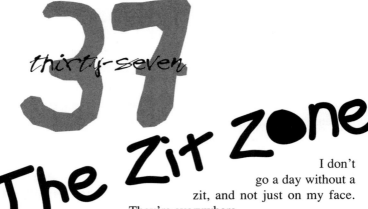

# 37

*thirty-seven*

# The Zit Zone

I don't go a day without a zit, and not just on my face. They're everywhere.

When I wake up in the morning, it looks like my face was up all night making pimples. How can I put an end to the annoying night shift? What's the fastest way to get an ugly red zit to take a hike?

Cyberspace has zits . . . *a whole web site dedicated to zits.* Amazing. You can download all sorts of information on whiteheads, blackheads, megazyborg zits, and those infamous "right-before-

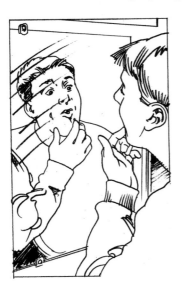

a-hot-date-third-eye-Cyclops-dead-center-on-your-forehead" zits from the OXY–5 web site (www.oxy-zone.com). As you can tell from the above students' questions, waking up in the morning and discovering your face is in the zit zone causes severe adolescent desperation. If fighting zits and acne is a daily problem, you probably wonder whether God is trying to play some sadistic joke on you. Like many other teenagers, you're not alone in asking, "God, are you listening to me? Are you there?"

When you are struggling with zits, your self-image, and wondering what other people think when they look at you, remind yourself that God does talk with you and listen to you through his Holy Spirit. **Read John 15:26–16:15.**

The Holy Spirit is tough for a lot of Christians (even adults) to figure out. Our modern culture with its emphasis on logical thought, practicality, and technology leaves little room for a supernatural being like the Holy Spirit. For some reason, it just seems too far-out to deal with. And the church doesn't help much when it depicts the Holy Spirit as a mystical ghost who helps superspiritual people. Nothing is more untrue.

God knew that people flounder because they cannot see God. So the Lord provided a *Comforter,* a *Counselor inside us.*

The Holy Spirit acts with our consciences, warning of attitudes or actions that will hurt us, or comforting us when we hurt. It is a mystery *how* God works in people who know him personally. The Bible says the world can't accept this mystery. There is a danger that Christians too can be influenced by the world to believe the Holy Spirit is unimportant.

If you have asked God to forgive you of your sins through the death of Jesus Christ for you, and you are walking with him as your Lord, God's Spirit is in you. This world will do whatever it can to discredit the Holy Spirit and his work in your life. Though your zits may not vanish for a long time, the Holy Spirit promises to remain always.

## Get a Grip

The Holy Spirit is sent by God to comfort and guide you, not freak you out. In what ways does the Spirit show that it is him speaking, instead of your imagination and wishes?

# 38

*thirty-eight*

# Gut Feelings

Guilt
Guilt
Guilt
Guilt

Guilt. You know what it feels like. Guilt is that paralyzing, acid-churning, sickening feeling in the pit of your stomach when you know you've done something wrong. The longer you avoid dealing with the guilt—that gut feeling that God is tugging on your heart—the worse it gets. Stealing. Lying. Cheating. Beating someone up. Premarital sex. Whatever you've done, your guilt isn't going to go away. Unless, of course, you decide to do something about it.

It would be untrue to say that doing what you know is wrong doesn't feel good at first—or that it isn't fun. But if you have truly accepted Christ into your heart, God's Spirit within you is hurt. It's as if he's been watching all along, and since he's an integral part of you, you feel uneasy over your sin.

**Read Psalm 32.** This psalm of David brings home what happens when we delay talking with God about sin. David pours out his thoughts in verses 3 and 4—his unconfessed sin had consequences. Once he admitted this, he knew God had forgiven him. He could once again have a good relationship with God. When you've hurt someone by something you've

84

said or done, don't you both feel an awkwardness that continues to get worse the longer you both ignore it?

The same is true in your relationship with God. If you keep ignoring what you know is separating you from him, it will only strain the relationship, and you will feel distant from God. If you feel that a wall has been erected between you and God, he is not the one who is responsible. Try talking to him about it, as you'd talk to a close friend. He wants to share your sorrow and your fear. If you continue to separate yourself from him through unconfessed sin, you're hurting yourself and you're also hurting God.

Get a Grip

Reflect on your relationship with God. Is everything straight between you and God, or are you hiding—or trying to hide—those guilty gut feelings from him?

Why does God allow you to feel those guilty gut feelings when you sin?

## thirty-nine
## 39
## Burnt Out

"I can't believe John calls himself a Christian," Denise snaps. "Did you see how drunk he was at Kim's house last Friday night? I liked him because I thought he was different than everyone else, but if *that* is what being a Christian is all about, I'm not sure if I want to go on your church's retreat. The last thing I want to be called is a 'hypocrite'!"

What are you supposed to say?

When was the last time someone else's less-than-Christian behavior created a tough conversation for you? You've been telling a friend about Christ, when you're smacked upside the head with the hypocrisy of someone in your youth group. Maybe you've even wondered deep inside your heart, *If that's what a Christian is, forget it.* Do you ever feel that other people's actions are burning out *your* relationship with God? If so, you're not alone.

**Take a moment to read 1 Corinthians 3.** Back when these words were written, some people in the church were rallying behind personalities—Christian superstars—and forgetting that the Christian faith rests on belief in God, not people. There have always been, and will always be, people in the church who claim to be Christians but don't live the life they profess. Sometimes they're even Christian leaders, like the religious leaders in Christ's time, the Pharisees.

None of us is perfect; we're all hypocrites in that we don't consistently live the God-dependence and purity of an authentic Christian lifestyle. We don't have to be perfect to be accepted by God. In fact, we need to admit our imperfections.

Keeping your eyes on people is one of the quickest ways to burn out on Christianity. Somehow it won't make much sense to someday stand before God and whine, "But God, there were so many hypocrites in the church!" He'll probably agree wholeheartedly and then ask the piercing question: "But what about you? I never asked you to put your faith in people, but in me."

What about you? Are you allowing other people to distance you from God? Are you confusing the wisdom of men with the power of God?

---

## Get a Grip

Don't let the actions of others burn out your relationship with God. What can you do to stay focused on him, not others?

---

# 40 forty
# Body Surfing

Basketball superstar Michael Jordan can do amazing aerial acrobat maneuvers with that pressurized, black-striped orange sphere. There is *something* that Jordan doesn't do well . . . swim.

Chicago Bulls center, Luc Longley, took a beating on the floor of the Pacific Ocean when he got in trouble body surfing on a road trip. Jordan told a coach they wouldn't have to worry about him doing it: "There's something about water that doesn't agree with me."

Can you believe it? "Air Jordan," the one person on planet earth who defies the laws of gravity, doesn't float. Even Michael Jordan has limitations.

Balance is one of the most important conditions we need to maintain in life. Like body surfing and basketball, there will be some things we can do and some things we can't do. Balance is a way to understand our limitations.

Without balance, gymnasts break their routines, wars start, people get the flu, fires break out, and banks are robbed. Throughout every area of life, balance is needed to insure quality, peace, and good health.

Balance is not often talked about among Christians. Yet the Bible is one long record of God working to bring balance to unbalanced people.

**Buried in the New Testament is a phenomenal little Scripture verse, Luke 2:52.** Notice how this verse breaks the life of Jesus into four parts: He grew in

| | |
|---|---|
| wisdom (mentally) | favor with God (spiritually) |
| stature (physically) | favor with people (socially) |

Jesus was growing in normal ways. Since Jesus is our model we can use these categories to measure our personal growth. Mental, physical, spiritual, and social growth are important to God. We will look at the importance of balance in each of these areas. Remember that God is committed to balance in your life just as he was in the growth of Jesus.

More than making you obey rules, God wants you to maintain balance in your life. Like body surfing, maintaining balance can be difficult when all you're doing is trying to keep your head above water. There are a lot of different things you could build your life on. But God's love and his ways are the absolute best foundation for a balanced life.

Get a Grip

Life balance is something you *maintain*—not something that you're born with or "just have." Have you invited God to help you with yours lately? What two or three areas in your life need the most help?

# 41
*forty-one*

## Mental Hula Hoops

*Memory Fuel.*
*Fast Blast. Energy Elick-*
*sure. Mind Mix.* These are some of the
"smart drinks." *Nootropics,* the mixing of drugs and
nutrients to produce memory and intelligence in the human
mind, is just another trendy and expensive way to stretch the
mind.

Popular at dance clubs, these drinks are mixed by savvy
entrepreneurs with an eye on making a buck by blending smart
drugs with juices and amino acids. The results are question-
able. As James McGaugh, director of the Center for the Neu-
robiology of Learning and Memory at the University of California at Irvine, said, "These smart drugs are nothing more
than a hula hoop for the mind."

You don't have to drink anything to improve the intelligence God has already given you. God is far more concerned
with what you put into your mind and what you think. **Read
Philippians 4:4–9.** If you could read this in the original language of the New Testament—Greek—you would see that

these verses encourage you to think good thoughts and to let those thoughts shape your *attitudes*. That's because *what* we think has a big impact on *how* we act.

Thinking correctly is a vital part of being a balanced person. Remember that Luke 2:52 said Jesus grew in wisdom, as well as physically. Jesus could never have done what he did unless he developed and used his mind correctly.

Do you want to be smart? Maybe you're getting good grades already, and you can hold your own in most any conversation with an adult. That is not what the Bible calls true wisdom. The Bible says respect for God is the beginning of wisdom. And this respect isn't related to how smart you are. It's something anyone can have.

In Philippians we get practical guidance on what to think about. This kind of thinking can keep you balanced, so that your mind doesn't become a garbage can for the latest thing the world is pushing. Garbage in, garbage out. Your mind is worth more, both to God and to you.

## Get a Grip

Think back to a situation when you got into trouble because your thoughts led you down the wrong road. What will you do next time those thoughts come?

# 42

*forty-two*

# Jesus unplugged

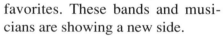

Every musician seems to have an acoustic album. Most of the legendary bands have either been on MTV's *Unplugged* or have cut their own informal, earthy-sounding acoustic album. *Led Zeppelin, Rod Stewart, Eric Clapton, Neil Young, Nirvana, The Eagles.* All of their "unplugged" versions of old classics put a new spin on these favorites. These bands and musicians are showing a new side.

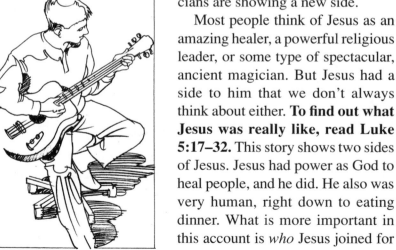

Most people think of Jesus as an amazing healer, a powerful religious leader, or some type of spectacular, ancient magician. But Jesus had a side to him that we don't always think about either. **To find out what Jesus was really like, read Luke 5:17–32.** This story shows two sides of Jesus. Jesus had power as God to heal people, and he did. He also was very human, right down to eating dinner. What is more important in this account is *who* Jesus joined for dinner. Pious Jews of the day (Pharisees) complained about who Jesus was eating with. These guys missed the whole point. They couldn't understand that Jesus was interested in giving such people—tax collectors, prostitutes, thieves—a new life.

Sometimes our mental picture of Jesus is too one-dimensional. The simple, even mysterious, fact is that Jesus was human. He had friends, many of whom did not believe as he did. What does this mean to you?

This takes balance. It matters *who* your friends are. You can't go through life just hanging out with Christians. However, neither can you be a consistent Christian if your strong friendships are with people who don't know God personally. Adults who caution you about your friends are right. The key is balance.

Be a person of conviction when you are with friends who don't know God. If they put you down, then your friendship isn't as important as you think. When you do things with your friends who don't know God, do safe things in neutral places. Their influence is stronger than you are, no matter what you think.

Friendships are important in life. Choose yours carefully and be careful what you do with them.

We need to show God's love to everyone we meet. But who you choose for close friends will help shape you.
Are you hangin' with people who build you up or tear you down?

# 43

## forty-three

## Artificial Life

As we head into the twenty-first century, we'll hear more about artificial life and artificial intelligence—computers programmed to mimic the fundamental processes and systems of living beings. Artificial life involves such wild concepts as robots, fuzzy logic, and nanotechnology (repeat *nanotechnology* five times as fast as you can).

Artificial life has severe limits. One is that it fails to address the spiritual side of our lives. Artificial life may be an interesting topic to discuss and explore, but it can't give us answers to life's big questions—and it can't give eternal life. If we ever hope to be everything that God has created us to be, we need the spiritual balance to the physical, social, and mental aspects of our lives.

**In Mark 12:28–34, Jesus gave two commands that can act as the spiritual keys we need:**

Love God with all your heart, soul, mind, and strength.
Love your neighbor as much as yourself.

Wrapped up in these two phrases is a spiritually balanced life. Let's take a closer look:

*Love God with all your heart (emotions), soul (beliefs), mind (mentally), and strength (body).* All the aspects we have been talking about—physical, mental, and now spiritual—are here. One key to being balanced spiritually is to bring all of you into the process of loving God. Take heart. That doesn't turn you into a religious fanatic who can only eat, sleep, breathe, and talk religion. God takes what we dedicate to him and points it at the real world in which we live. He sees you as a whole person, not a "soul."

*Love your neighbor as yourself.* Here is the social side of us. God expects us to spend time with all types of people and to show love for them all, including our families.

As you seek after the eternal life God has for you in Jesus Christ, spiritual balance will come in your life. Be patient with yourself and with God. As you work to apply these commands and to stay balanced in the other areas of your life, God promises to help in the process. You won't have to rely on a computer for artificial life. You can depend on the Author of eternal life.

Get a Grip

What is a practical way to love God with all of your heart, soul, mind, and strength today?

# 44 forty-four

# The Mask

In the movie *The Mask*, actor Jim Carrey's pea-green face, ultra-bright teeth, mile-long tongue, and googly eyeballs covered his real feelings. The movie's message is that all of us are dying to be someone else in some parts of our lives. That's why we wear masks in the first place.

To varying degrees, we all wear masks. We hide behind them with our real feelings and thoughts. Masks generally do more harm than good. God's perfect plan is to free you to be yourself—all the time. Unfortunately, sin has altered God's perfect plan, so we struggle with masks that disguise the truth. **Ephesians 4:17–32 has something helpful to say about masks.**

Masks can come in many shapes. People try to act smarter, richer, or more popular than they really are.

> If you get turned down for a date but tell your friends it doesn't matter—that's wearing a mask.
> If you go out with your friends to do something that you feel inside is wrong—that's wearing a mask.

Masks hide our convictions, feelings, personalities, and Christianity from others. Are you lying to others by wearing a mask? The Bible says to stop lying to each other. That is a call to start to be honest with yourself and others. You may need a little practice at first, especially if you've had some mask on for a while. Ask God to help you.

The more honest you are with others about the real you, the more you will feel like a whole person. Unlike Jim Carrey, you won't have to worry about your face turning green or anyone stepping on your tongue.

### Get a Grip

What mask do you sometimes wear?
Since some masks hide you from yourself, these may be particularly hard to spot.
Are there masks that would feel soooo good to take off?

97

# 45 forty-five

# Happy or Holy?

*God wants me to be happy.* This is just one of the many myths of modern-day Christianity.

Another myth is that God will answer every and any prayer—*prayers for a new girlfriend or boyfriend . . . prayers for an "A" on the test you didn't study for . . . prayers for more money so you can buy the right kind of cool clothing to stay in style with everyone else.* Despite what we or many other people may think, God does not exist to make us happy. The story of Jonah is a perfect example. **Take time to read the short book of Jonah.**

Anyone with even a nodding acquaintance with the Bible has heard how Jonah disobeyed God and was thrown into the sea and swallowed by a great fish. The reason he disobeyed was that God sent him to warn a people he absolutely hated. God told him to tell the people in the city of Nineveh that they would be destroyed because of their sin. It was not an easy thing to do. Often in our lives doing the right thing is not easy or comfortable.

Jonah should have felt good after the people listened to him and turned from their sin. Instead, he was ticked. He felt so mad he wanted to die. He wanted to nuke the Ninevites. Jonah didn't understand why God was being kind to them. He didn't notice God's kindness to him. God wanted Jonah to trust him in all things. We don't know at the end of the story whether Jonah learned anything from his experience. He must have, since he or another prophet wrote it down for us.

What about you? Are you willing to do what you know God wants you to, even when the results don't go your way? You may have to go the extra mile with your parents for a while, without seeing them ease up on you. It may mean giving up friends who are bad influences on you, even without any friends in sight to take their place. In the long run it will always pay off to do what God's Word says. However, in the short run it helps to remember that walking with God doesn't mean we'll always be happy or comfortable. Jonah certainly wasn't happy with everything God told him to do, but ultimately, Jonah evidently decided that following God's plan for holiness was best. If you want true, lasting joy and not temporary happiness, set your heart on holiness—going God's way more and more and your way less and less.

Ask God to help you today with your point of view.
Following God may not always make you happy.
What is one practical way to practice holiness today?

# 46 forty-six

# keeping His Promise

If convenience stores are open 24 hours a day, 365 days a year, why do they have locks on the door?

Why do mattresses have warning labels? Do you *really* get in trouble if you pull them off?

If nothing sticks to Teflon, then how does Teflon stick to the pan?

Why do girls always go to the bathroom in groups, and why do guys communicate in grunts and shrugs?

Why do parents act like zombies when you ask to borrow ten bucks?

These are perplexing questions. As Christians, there are also a lot of things we don't understand about God. In fact, we often have a one-sided view of God. Since we can never understand totally what he's about, the most we can do is look at who he is through ways he has interacted with people in the Bible, and how he has revealed himself to us personally. But even then, it's hard to understand how he can judge our sin on one hand and be a loving Father on the other. Most of us know what it's like to be punished or judged, but few of us have really experienced pure unconditional love.

**Read Romans 8:35–39 and its list of things that can't separate us from God's love.** Not life, not death, not angels, not the powers of hell, not your fears, not your worries, not even if you're in an airplane or a submarine.

Did you notice that "sin" is not included on the list? Though a Christian cannot "lose" salvation, sin does separate us from the closeness God desires. We are not separated from the love of God. If you feel alone or have failed again in a certain area, remember this promise—nothing can separate you from the love of God. You can count on him to forgive you and to be with you today and forever. In this confusing world, the one thing you can trust in and understand is that God always keeps his promises. His doors are always open, and there are no locks.

God has never broken any promise found in the
   Bible—ever. Those promises are for you, too.
   Do you trust him?
Can you name a promise God has kept in your life?
Does that memory help you to trust him more, even
   when God seems to be on vacation?

# 47

forty-seven

# The Price of Popularity

A friend goes out for the football team, a club, or has a prestigious new honor. All of a sudden, your friend is a totally different person. Your phone calls are not returned. Answers to questions about plans for the weekend are vague. He doesn't join you at lunch anymore; he's sitting down with a "new" crew of friends. Suddenly, you're a half-eaten bologna sandwich.

If you're feeling alone and ignored because of a former friend's newfound popularity, or if you're popular and want to know how to keep things balanced, read how popularity changed the way some people behaved in Jesus' time. Popularity problems have been around for a long time. As you probably know, the price of popularity can be a bit high. **Read John 12:37–50.**

In the case of the Jewish leaders, respect and praise mattered more than what they believed. It mattered so much that they compromised their honesty. Pushing for popularity can do the same thing to you. It's good to have friends, but whenever finding friends and looking for their praise takes your focus off important things in life, then things have gone too far.

In the same way, if you are tempted to compromise to stay popular, your life is out of balance. Balance is the key, and God can help you get it and maintain it. But the price of balance is not cheap. Check the balance in your life. Fewer activities, attending fewer parties, and learning to be comfortable alone may be in order.

Friendships and the respect of people are important. Having the friendship and respect of God is more important. There's always a cost for popularity, but popularity comes and goes. Friendship with God lasts forever. What it costs is all of you.

## Get a Grip

What price have you paid in seeking friends?
If someone asked God if you were his friend and how good a friend you are, what would he say?

# X Games

The X Games were developed as ESPN's radical alternative to the Olympic Games. They are the insanest, adrenaline-pumping, extreme sports you can imagine: skateboarding, skysurfing, sport climbing, street luge racing, bungee jumping, barefoot water-ski jumping, bicycle half-pipe competitions. TV viewers are presented the very best in these alternative sports.

The X Games have a definite, rebellious edge to them. These extreme sports are radical. They push the limits. They challenge the conventional sports. Many of these sports reflect the hard-core, push-the-limits, rebellious nature of men and women. Like the X Games, we sometimes want to be different, unique, playing by our own rules, rebelling against God. We want to find a new alternative.

Rebellion is in everyone. After you become a Christian, rebellion still raises its head. **To see how God**

**looks at rebellion, read Luke 15:11–32.** Rebellion has consequences. The lost son spent his money, got quite hungry, and felt so low he went and took a job feeding pigs. But the story doesn't end there. The son made a choice to come back, not knowing exactly how his family would respond. His smart choice to live differently paid off.

And the choice to leave a rebellious spirit or attitude behind will pay off for you too. God is not going to condemn you for wrestling with rebellion. However, he is vitally concerned about how you channel rebellion into something constructive.

Throughout your life you will co-exist with rebellion. But as you let God control your life more and more, you will begin to see ways in which you can use that desire for change for something useful. The church needs people who can channel their desire for change into new music, drama, strong leadership, and relevant thinking.

Rebellion in your life can be an asset or a liability. It all depends on who you go to extremes for, yourself or God. It all depends on whether or not you want to play games with God.

## Get a Grip

Why does your rebellion break God's heart?
Think about one area of life in which you want to go your own way. Share it with a friend who can pray for you and hold you accountable.

# 49
## forty-nine
## High-Tech Truth

Have you noticed how major companies have tried to embrace spiritual themes for their print and television ad campaigns? IBM produced television ads showing Hindu monks meditating. The caption at the bottom of the screen had a double reference to the Hindu symbol and Lotus Software Company: "IBM and Lotus in spiritual harmony." Another IBM ad has depicted a couple giddy Italian nuns talking about their recent exploits surfing the net.

Though companies and ad agencies may use spiritual words or concepts, they are presenting their version of spiritual truth to make a buck. Everyone has an angle on truth and spirituality. It can be hard to get a handle on what the *real truth* is.

Paul wrote a letter to a young friend, Timothy, that talked about how to handle the information in our lives. **Read 2 Timothy 3.** These verses are really appropriate for our day. What is really interesting about this letter to Timothy is that it probably is one of the last letters Paul wrote. Paul used one of his last letters to a friend to tell him that God's Word is important and useful in helping us live our lives.

There is something to learn from this. God's Word is important in our lives. Without it, especially in today's information-packed world, we have little or no hope for making sense out of life. There's just too much out there to try to figure out.

How regularly are you reading God's Word? It's not how much you read or how long you think about it that counts. The chances of you keeping your head together are slim unless you are regularly exposed to reality and truth. God's Word can help you in life. If your Bible reading is irregular or only occasional you need to reevaluate just how important the Bible is to you. Set a reasonable goal for yourself so you read more this week than last. You'll find that God's Word can give you the help you need. God doesn't have to market truth. He is truth.

## Get a Grip

What is the one thing that consistently seems to keep you from getting alone with God and his Word? What can you do this week to sidestep this obstacle? Ask God to help.

# 50

fifty

# A Blockbuster

Gripping,
hand-to-hand,
bloody battle scenes.
Passionate, illicit sex. Intrigue,
betrayal, and conspiracy. Families
divided by jealousy, lies, and government coups. Sorcery, witchcraft, and demons.

And you thought the Bible was boring. The latest Hollywood blockbuster hit has nothing on the action-packed adven-
tures found in God's Word. "Well, what about special effects?"
you ask. Water flowing out of a solid rock. Fire from heaven
consuming animal sacrifices. Raging seas stilled in a second.
A small girl rising from the dead. How's that for starters?

Sometimes you feel guilty and think something's wrong
with your walk with God if the Bible doesn't grab you as did
the latest movie. The Bible is packed with exciting stories,
but once you've read them a few times, don't feel weird if you
get bored. It's normal to have times when the Bible reads like
any other book.

**For more insight on what to do when your Bible reading
just isn't working, read Deuteronomy 6:1–9.** It's not very
obvious at first, but in this chapter is an angle on the problem

of dry Bible reading. You'll notice God told the Jewish people to impress his commands on their children, to talk about them everywhere, to tie them to their hands (or memorize them), and to write them on the door (communicate them to others). What was the point of all this? Two things are important.

First, God seems to be saying that variety is good when it comes to learning his Word. There is no set way to have your devotions. If you are sharper in the morning, then read in the morning. If you want to read out loud to a friend or someone in your family, that's okay too. No law says you have to read the Bible a certain way or at a certain time of the day.

Second, there's an old saying: "This Book [the Bible] will keep you from sin; sin will keep you from this Book." God's Word is valuable and can correct our bad thinking and instruct us on how to live a holy life in today's crazy world. But sin can keep us from getting the most from the Bible.

If you are serious about being a Christian, you can't ignore God's Word. Unlike Hollywood's blockbuster hits, the Bible has stood the test of time. God's Word can make your life a blockbuster hit.

Get a Grip

Why is it important to read God's Word even when you don't feel like it?

Next time your Bible reading gets boring, ask God to help you. Check your life out. Then try some variety.

# 51

*fifty-one*

# Riding the Fence

"What time did you get in last night?" your dad asks you as you sit down at the breakfast table on a Saturday morning.

"Oh, a little after eleven," you say in a confident voice. You hope the conversation will stop here.

"Eleven, huh? That's funny. . . . I was up until midnight reading, and I never heard you come in."

"Well, you see . . . when I said, 'after eleven' what I really meant was. . . ."

You know he's got you. Cancel your plans for the rest of the weekend. No, make that your life. You're busted!

Certain things just do not mix in life. The Bible talks about two such attitudes that are on opposite sides of the fence. If you want to be all that God has designed you to be, there's no way you can be riding the fence between his way and the world's way. **Read about these two attitudes in James 4:1–17.**

The Bible is clear—being friends with the evil pleasures of the world makes you an enemy of God. This is not easy or fun to hear. But it is true.

Some of the most unhappy and frustrated Christians are those who try to party on Friday and Saturday nights and then show up for church on Sunday mornings. It just doesn't work. Christianity requires our concentrated commitment. It is not designed for people who are undecided about its value. This doesn't mean we have to be reclusive and hide away from the world. It doesn't mean that life has to be one long prayer meeting. It *does* mean that the value system of a Christian is different. Having a good time, dressing well, and partying with lots of friends have their place in a Christian's life, but not the *same* place as in the life of someone who doesn't know the Lord. The Christian's motivation, attitude, and actions are going in a different direction than those of the world. This is especially true when it comes to the sorts of things that give pleasure.

Are you trying to have a good time God's way *and* the world's way? It won't work. Put your whole commitment into doing things God's way, and you'll see some of the pieces of your life start to fit together. Riding the fence isn't worth it. Do you want to live with frustration or peace?

Get a Grip

In what ways do you sometimes ride the fence between God's way and the world's way?

# 52
## fifty-two
## Call 911

It's a billion-dollar business, and using it is way more expensive than your average long-distance phone call. The cost cannot be computed merely in dollars. Calling 900 numbers often means seeking *phone sex*. It's as easy as punching in eleven buttons on the telephone, giving a credit card number, and slipping off into a sexual fantasy never-never-land. For an outrageous $3 or $4 a minute, lots of guys are lured to believe that this crazy form of "audio intimacy" is harmless.

If you're tempted to dial a 900 number, call God's 911 number instead.

How would you rate your self-discipline when it comes to battling sexual or other temptations? Are you winning more than you're losing? Losing more battles than you're winning? If you have never dialed a 900 number, you may struggle against other temptations. Maybe you can honestly say you haven't been tempted for some time. Sometimes temptation is very clear. Other times, it's not. Shoplifting or having sex outside marriage or damaging others' property are easy to spot as wrong. Other rights and wrongs aren't so defined and are more easily rationalized. **Read 1 Corinthians 10:1–14, considering how to handle temptation when it comes.**

Sometimes God doesn't have to discipline us for sin—we discipline and even punish ourselves. At the time, it's easier to give in and do what we want, but we usually pay for it. Embarrassment, guilt, hurt, broken relationships, even death, can result when we give in to temptation.

When Jesus died on the cross, he broke the *power* of sin in your life. How this works is still a mystery to man. The important thing to remember is that while the *power* of sin in your life was broken by Jesus' death, you will still sin. No man or woman will ever die having completely beaten sin. This doesn't mean we should give up and give in to temptation. It *does* mean that God wants to help us get our batting averages up and give in to temptation less and less.

What makes it difficult to call on God when you are tempted?
Ask God to help you hear his voice clearly when you are tempted. God can guide your thoughts and conscience to help you escape.

# 53

fifty-three

## Losing My Religion

Stupid rituals. Doubts. Too many "do's and don'ts." Religious hypocrisy. Sin. Lifestyle choices. Peer pressure. Confusion. These are a few of the reasons teenagers give for rejecting a relationship with Jesus Christ. Many young people think following Jesus means that they have to become "religious." They think God is a kind of demented Santa Claus, a cosmic and ruthless tyrant who keeps a daily tally on what they do or don't do.

Well, God does keep a record of our lives but not in the way you and I commonly think. **To find out exactly what kind of spiritual scorecard God keeps, read Psalm 103:9–18 and Luke 10:20.**

These verses in Psalm 103 tell you what God *doesn't* put on your record—your sins. The Bible says God doesn't bear a grudge or remain angry forever. He has moved our sin away from us as far as east is from west—in other words, a distance that defies measurement. You may have noticed that God moves the sin away from *you*. Why? Because God loves you as a person but hates the sin in your life. Separating you from your sin by more miles than you can measure guarantees God will never see you and your sin together. It guarantees complete forgiveness. The record kept is whether your name is registered as a citizen of heaven. But you have to make the decision. Such concepts as whether your name is recorded in heaven seem off-the-wall, particularly in a world obsessed with what can be seen and experienced. But the concept *is* real. Your whole hope of living after you die is tied to this concept. The Bible has made it clear that when people come to Christ for forgiveness of sins their names *are* recorded in heaven.

Do you have confidence that your name is recorded in God's book of life in heaven? Or have you been playing religious games? Maybe you've been faking your Christianity for so long that you've fooled even yourself. Maybe it's time for you to lose your religion by developing a real relationship with Jesus. Knowing God personally is your only hope for a meaningful life and living forever. He's waiting to hear from you. Take some time today, right now, to lose your religion and gain a relationship that will last forever.

## Get a Grip

How does it make you feel knowing that God throws all your sins as far as east is from west? If you know that you've been playing games with God or not taking the sin in your life seriously, go ahead and talk to God about it right now.

# 54 fifty-four

# It's NOT My Job!

"If I hear you whine or complain one more time," your mom snaps at you, her glasses steaming with a menacing mist, "you're going to be in big trouble! I'm sick and tired of your attitude about helping around this house!"

"But it's not my job. I took out the trash last week. It's that little, lazy doofus's turn to do something around here for once," you retort with a squinting-evil-eyes glare at your lower-life-form younger sister.

"I don't care if it's her week to take out the trash. . . . I asked YOU to do it!"

You think, *And what if I don't?*

Ooouummph . . . Dooonn't aaaask thaaaat question!

Chores are a part of living. Always have been. Always will be. How is your attitude about chores? **Read what the Bible says about attitude in 1 Peter 3:10–17.** These verses give you a formula for a happy attitude toward life:

Keep control of your tongue. (Do your chores without complaining.)

Don't tell lies. (Are they *really* done?)

Turn away from evil. (Be honest. Do them when you are told to.)

Live in peace, even if you have to chase it. (Accept the criticism and the praise when it comes.)

It takes a lot of energy to keep a house going and in order. Sometimes parents can get so busy that they assign chores without thinking about your tests or date. The same formula that will help you handle the chores will also help you work out the differences. By sitting down and being reasonable (controlling your tongue and doing your best to keep peace), you will demonstrate an attitude that is pleasing to your parents and to God.

Get a Grip

How's your attitude about serving others (yes, even your family)?

# 55

fifty-five

# Next Steps

The Christian life is often compared to a long journey filled with roadblocks, setbacks, peaceful rest stops, bumpy roads, and uphill climbs. Along this road we travel with Christ, the path before us is solid, but seldom smooth. When you hike high in the mountains, at or above the tree line, you travel steep, difficult, narrow trails that are physically challenging. A high-altitude hike puts strain on your body and finds all the weak spots in your muscles.

The Achilles tendon in your lower leg gets its name from the Greek soldier who was supposedly immune to enemy wounds except in his heel, the anchor point for this tendon. An arrow hit him in—you guessed it—the heel. If you ever pulled that tendon in sports you know how Achilles felt. It can be a painful injury.

We all have areas of weakness in our lives ("Achilles tendons") that can be spiritually injured if we're not careful where we step. For some reason everyone's personality is predisposed to some kind of besetting sin or repeated failure. **Read Romans 7:15–25 for some insight into protecting and strengthening these vulnerable areas.**

Sometimes we get the impression that men and women mentioned in the Bible were spiritual giants who didn't struggle in life as we do. These verses should put that myth to rest. Paul gets down to some honest, gut-level communication. Whatever it was, Paul's struggle went with him. Like all who want to please God with a holy life, he found himself sometimes beaten by sin in his life.

As long as we live, we struggle with sin. As you get older, what tempts you might change. Whatever it is, its power was broken when Christ died on the cross. But you will still sin. With Paul, we have to turn to Christ to rescue us.

As a Christian, you have important choices to make about what trails to travel in life. There will always be opportunities to give in to temptation. Use your head and stay out of situations in which you are easily tempted. Call on God often for help. Remember that Jesus is walking beside you, in front of you, and behind you. All along the way, his Spirit will comfort you, encourage you, prod you when you're tired, and give you the rest you need when you feel like you can't take another step. Walk with Jesus. He's walking with you.

## Get a Grip

What is the next step on the trail God is asking you to take?

Your weaknesses are also opportunities for learning to depend on God and helping others who are going through similar problems. How might God use the worst tragedy or failure of your life?